WILTSHIRE

A century in photographs

Published jointly by
Wiltshire Federation of
Women's Institutes and
Countryside Books

First published 1998

COUNTRYSIDE BOOKS
3 Catherine Road
Newbury, Berkshire

ISBN 1 85306 538 2
Designed by Graham Whiteman

Produced through MRM Associates Ltd., Reading
Printed by Borcombe Printers plc, Romsey

Foreword

'Everything has changed since I was a girl'. 'Nothing ever changes around here'. How often do we hear these contradictory cries?

Wiltshire has changed in the last hundred years. Many more roads and much more traffic to snarl up towns and cause pollution. Fewer trains, stations lost forever, but the rivers are still there and the canals are making a comeback even if it is only for leisure purposes.

The villages have no blacksmith or baker, often no shop or post office but cricket and football are still played on village greens throughout the county.

The towns have spread out into the countryside with thousands of houses and large populations. Yet much of the land continues to be farmed albeit by modern methods and by growing different crops.

The Army remains ensconced on Salisbury Plain – the cavalry has gone but the tanks are there instead.

Much has changed, and yet – go down that little lane, turn the next corner and still can be found the picturesque villages and hamlets our forefathers knew. Beautiful buildings, ancient woods, valleys and downs as they have been for centuries.

This book provides an insight into the old and the new. Each photograph from the early part of the century matched by another from its dying years. They illustrate the changes and the continuity.

I hope that for everyone who reads the book some memory is stirred or an interest aroused in this beautiful county.

So very different yet so very much the same!

Kathy Wright
Federation Chairman

All Cannings Village Shop

Spanning the century, the building that housed All Cannings' post office and shop in the early 1900s is today the village hall. Goods were delivered around the local area in the Pewsey Vale by horse and cart every week, and the shop provided nearly everything required for everyday living. A trip to town would have been a luxury for many people.
(Cynthia Luffman – All Cannings, Etchilhampton & Allington WI)

All Cannings Village Shop

The building was purchased from the Cavendish Land Company in 1914 by an elderly spinster. It was to be used by the men of the parish as a refuge, for reading, games and, it's said, to escape the nagging tongues of the village wives! After use as a grain store during the Second World War, it became the first meeting place of the village Women's Institute in 1948. In 1971 it was converted into the village hall, the central meeting place for the parish.
(Cynthia Luffman – All Cannings, Etchilhampton & Allington WI)

The Baker at Ashton Keynes

At the turn of the century there were three bakers at Ashton Keynes, all making their own bread and cakes and delivering them around the village. This was Mr Payne (*left*), with the tricycle he used to get about – although the method of carrying the bread leaves a lot to be desired! Today things have changed. A part-time assistant sells bread made commercially (*right*), from the only remaining general store in the village.
(Margaret Goldsmith, Ivan Webster – Ashton Keynes WI)

AVEBURY VILLAGE STREET

Unlike many villages which have been infilled, Avebury has lost buildings since the turn of the century. Several were demolished in the 1940s and 1950s by the National Trust, including the thatched cottages in the middle of the picture and the reading room. Today (*inset*) the scene is very different. The horse and cart once carried beer barrels from Butlers Brewery in West Kennett, but the new pub sign shows it now belongs to Whitbread.
(Joan Greenaway – Avebury & District WI)

Baydon Village Street

The old Roman road of Ermin Street leads up through the north-east tip of Wiltshire into Baydon, the county's highest inhabited village. In this photograph from the turn of the century, the farms along the roadside indicate the main employment of this closely knit community. The thatched cottages on the right housed one of the many small village shops, and beyond was the public house.
(Penny Stephens – Baydon WI)

Baydon Village Street

Ermin Street was widened in 1960 to accommodate the increasing volume of road traffic, and to provide a 'haul' road for the motorway construction that was then beginning. The M4 now snakes its way around the village providing easy access to outside work. The garage built on the site of the old poultry farm benefits from motorway recovery work. The shop now incorporates the cottages, and the Red Lion pub is still there serving the community.
(Penny Stephens – Baydon WI)

Biddestone Village Pond

Biddestone's village pond was well used earlier in the century. In addition to providing drinking water for animals, water was taken from the pond for use in steam engines passing through the village, and during hot spells wooden-wheeled waggons would drive in to soak for a while so that the iron bands on the wheels would not come loose. In winter villagers skated here, though even then an area was kept clear of ice so the animals could drink.
(Sheila Blake, Gareth Jacques – Biddestone & Hartham WI)

Biddestone Village Pond

Today the pond is a tourist attraction and less water flows into it. Biddestone itself is a very different place – the shop/post office and the school have closed, while cottages have been renovated or enlarged. Two small housing developments were built in the 1960s. The old self-sufficient village is gone, but it is still a very popular place to live and to visit, with two public houses on and near the green. Only ducks use the village pond today!
(Sheila Blake, Elvina Taylor – Biddestone & Hartham WI)

Outside Bishopstone Mill

A Sunday school outing in 1900, with a waggon drawn by two bullocks. The mill at Bishopstone would have been working then with its great waterwheel still in place at the side. Everyone is in their Sunday best and the girls all wear hats and white pinafores over their dresses, while the boys wear knickerbockers and caps. There are a lot of grown ups too, to enjoy the fun and keep the children in order.
(Paul Williams, via Bishopstone & Hinton Parva WI)

Outside Bishopstone Mill

Today's photograph shows the village schoolchildren once again outside the mill, which is now a private residence. This time they are with a more modern conveyance! They wear their school uniforms or casual clothes and are much more relaxed and exuberant than their predecessors in the face of the camera. So much change has taken place but village children still go to the local school and the mill building still stands.
(Penny Alston – Bishopstone & Hinton Parva WI)

Bowerchalke

When this photograph was taken at the turn of the century, the three houses of Providence Terrace, as it was named when it was built in 1876, yielded a total rental income of £12 per annum. The horse-drawn furniture van from a local railway station was probably expected by the people just visible at one of the doorways on the right.

(Sheila Collins – Bowerchalke WI)

Bowerchalke

Today, doors and windows have been freely exchanged on the little terrace to provide a single household named Summerfield, the home since 1968 of the Misses Bisset. The neighbouring cottage has lost its thatch but is still recognisably the same building. The modern removal van was kindly provided by Johnstones Removals of Salisbury, and illustrates well the change over the century in our mode of transport!
(Sheila Collins – Bowerchalke WI)

Box Market Place

At the turn of the century barrels of beer were being delivered by horse and dray in Box Market Place, and the children were dressed for the occasion to pose for the photographer. Today (*inset*) the railings have all gone and the corner shop has been converted into retirement flats. Cars have replaced the horses and children no longer feel safe to play in the street. But the Chequers Inn remains for local people and a small village work force.
(Helen Ellis – Box WI)

The Road to Box

The early medieval road through Box came down Quarry Hill, in the upper right distance, and up the right fork to meet what is now the main A4. In the earlier photograph, the left-hand road was known as Wharf Road. Many cottages have been demolished to make way for today's supermarket, and a garage forecourt, traffic signs, a telephone box and lots of traffic point to the obvious changes over the century.

(Maggie Roberts – Boxlea WI)

Boyton Bridge

Boyton Bridge straddles the River Wylye, carrying traffic to Codford and beyond. The old bridge was built in the late 1800s, but since then it has twice been rebuilt and the river diverted slightly. The thatched barns alongside the road and the house over the bridge survive. This is still a farming community, proud of its herd of rare Tamworth pigs which can often be seen, doing what pigs do, in the fields that border the sleepy backwater road to Cortington.
(Hazel Bryant – Cortington WI)

Bremhill Village Street

Bremhill is a small village that has not outwardly changed a lot over the years, many of its houses being listed. The post office and shop, school, resident vicar and regular bus service are all now gone, and the two farmhouses have been sold off. The school is the village hall in this close-knit community. In the main street the old well survives, which served the villagers before mains water was put in.

(Nancy Kyte, Linda Summers – Bremhill WI)

Brinkworth School

Brinkworth school was built in 1868, a little down the hill from the church. Village children received all their schooling here, unless they were able to go to Malmesbury Grammar School. In this quiet scene, the marks on the dusty road made by the wheels of horse-drawn carts can be clearly seen.

(Rosemary Tuck – Brinkworth WI)

Brinkworth School

After the Second World War the school continued as a primary school, and more recently it has been federated with Dauntsey Earl Danby's school. It now takes only juniors, and the infants are taught at Dauntsey. New permanent classrooms have been provided and the original building is today used as an assembly hall, library, staff room and offices. The old schoolmaster's house is occupied by the school caretaker.

(Rosemary Tuck – Brinkworth WI)

The Bell Inn, Bromham

The Bell Inn is at St Edith's Marsh, Bromham, at the side of what was once a quiet country road (quiet enough for the shepherd to let his sheep rest for a while) but is today the busy A342. There was also a water pump by the side of the building, which has now gone, and many more trees than there are today. The little cottage just to be seen on the left was burned down about 30 years ago.

(Betty McKendrick – Bromham WI)

Brunton, Collingbourne Kingston

Brunton is one of the three 'hamlets' that make up Collingbourne Kingston, the others being Kingston and Aughton. The gentleman on the steps in the old photo was the local coal merchant, and next door led to Brunton's shop and bakery. Oh, the smell of the lardy cakes! Today there are no shops. Village life is so changed. This was a no-through road, and just round the bend led to rolling downs and lanes.
(Mary Chandler – Collingbourne Kingston WI)

Burbage Village Street

In 1907 there was little traffic in Burbage's High Street and it was safe for the children who gathered there. The little thatched cottage on the right looks in very poor condition, and of course there were no amenities. Running water, electricity in the cottage homes, efficient heating and lighting, indoor toilets, all were far in the future for the villagers.
(Sheila Russell – Burbage WI)

Burbage Village Street

Today many changes are apparent in the street. The road is wider, properties have been renovated and rethatched, and the wires that bring us telephones and television are very noticeable. The road became very busy, taking a lot of the traffic for Salisbury, but since a bypass was built in 1991 it has been a great deal quieter – more like 1907! Yet the community is still growing, with new housing estates and a new school.
(Sheila Russell – Burbage WI)

CHIPPENHAM MARKET PLACE

In 1909 cattle were driven on the hoof up Chippenham High Street, along the old Bath to London coaching road, to the market place every week. Bulls were tethered to posts in the market place and occasionally one would break away, scattering the onlookers and scaring the children. Water could be got from the drinking fountain, with its gas light on top. It was a busy, noisy day of business and socialising.
(Pam Affleck – Hardenhuish WI)

Chippenham Market Place

The cattle market is still held every Friday, but has moved away from the old market place. Several buildings have been demolished, exposing the original half-timbered Yelde Hall which houses a museum. The drinking fountain has been converted into a war memorial on one side, leaving half the old fountain on the other, though its use is long forgotten. The high street has been bypassed and pleasantly pedestrianised.
(Pam Affleck – Hardenhuish WI)

Christian Malford lies by the River Avon in the Dauntsey Vale. This photograph was taken in front of the Mermaid Inn in 1926, of children and adults in fancy dress for the parade at the village fete. The band waits behind the group. The inn was unmodernised and the extension on the right dated back to the days when customers arrived by horse and trap. On each side of the old inn sign is a mounting block for riders.
(Susan Ault – Christian Malford & Foxham WI)

The Mermaid Inn, Christian Malford

It is a very different scene today at the Mermaid. The old stable block was burned down some 20 years ago and not replaced, the inn sign has been moved, and a large car park proclaims the needs of modern travel. This is a thriving community, with local people using the nearby M4 to travel far and wide to work, and as well as the Mermaid Inn the village can boast a shop and a school.
(Susan Ault – Christian Malford & Foxham WI)

Codford Railway Station

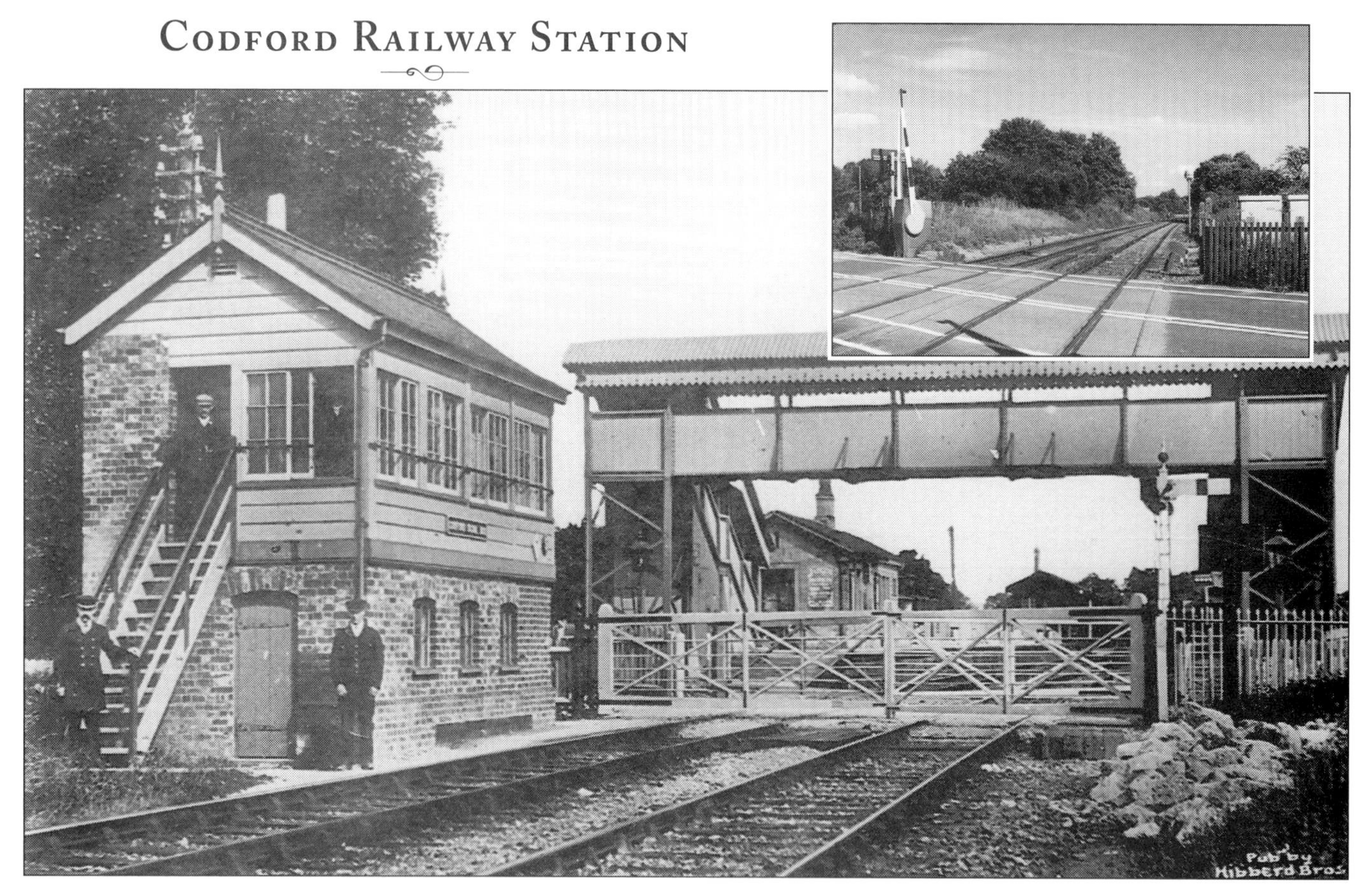

Until 1962 Codford had its own railway station, serving most of the villages of the Wylye valley and beyond. Located at the very edge of Codford on the border with Boyton and down in the valley, it employed 23 people in its heyday. Today *(inset)* the only remaining feature is the level crossing, now controlled by automatic barriers rather than the large wooden track gates. Local people have tried to get the station reopened but with no success.
(Hazel Bryant – Cortington WI)

Codford Village Street

Codford is a very old village and still has many old properties despite the modern expansion that has taken place. This photograph of Chitterne Road was taken when there was an ox's yard on the left, with granaries balanced up on staddle-stones. The house on the left was burned down and a Tudor-style house built in its place. The cottages on the right were thatched – so very different to today (*inset*).
(Sue Poolman – Codford WI)

The Last Straw in the ancient downland village of Collingbourne Ducis began life as a small farmhouse and there has been a building on the site since at least the 17th century. In the 1870s it became the village police station and the doorway on the far right was put in as an entrance to the police cells. Then early in the 1930s it became a private dwelling.

(Pamela Coydell – Collingbourne Kingston WI)

Today The Last Straw is almost unrecognisable from that cottage in the earlier photograph. In the early 1950s it became the Sally Lunn Tea Rooms and later The Last Straw public house. An extension was added in 1970 providing a restaurant area and in 1984 the timber-framed building was listed Grade II. Collingbourne Ducis today straddles the busy A338 road between Marlborough and Salisbury.
(Pamela Coydell – Collingbourne Kingston WI)

Corsley: Whitbourne Moor

Whitbourne Moor is a hamlet in the parish of Corsley and in the 19th century cloth making was carried out here, the mill employing people from Corsley and nearby. By the beginning of the 1900s, the majority of the cottages were inhabited by people working in agriculture and for the Longleat Estate. Today (*right*) most are privately owned and the inhabitants are retired or work outside the hamlet.

(Joy Snelgrove – Corsley WI)

CORSLEY: THE ROYAL OAK

The Royal Oak inn is situated on the A362 Frome to Warminster road and has been licensed since 1749, though it was built over 400 years ago. It is said to be haunted by the ghost of a young monk, from the time when it served as a rest house for travelling monks. Today it is modernised and has a restaurant but otherwise there is very little change from the days when the Wylye Valley Foxhounds met outside.
(Joy Snelgrove – Corsley WI)

Cortington Old Post Office

Lying between the villages of Boyton and Tytherington, Cortington (or more informally, 'Corton') nestles in the westerly end of the Wylye valley. The old post office closed in the late 1940s, and when this photograph was taken in the early years of the century the village also boasted a policeman, a school, three pubs, an undertaker, a blacksmith, one or two dairies and, if local tales are to be believed, a few houses of doubtful reputation!

(Hazel Bryant – Cortington WI)

Cortington Old Post Office

Today the old post office, still thatched and clearly recognisable from earlier in the century, is in residential use. The community has decreased over the years and Cortington is now a dormitory village with only a public house remaining from all those earlier institutions.
(Hazel Bryant – Cortington WI)

CRICKLADE HIGH STREET

Much has changed in Cricklade since the 1890s when this photograph was taken. In 1897 a clock was erected to celebrate Queen Victoria's Diamond Jubilee, and in those days the street was lit by gas lamps. Calcutt Street, coming in from the right, has been widened. Gone is the horse-drawn transport and also the need for the water pump at the roadside. Nor do cars leave their droppings!

(Sandra Samways – Cricklade WI)

Cricklade High Street

However, the first impression at looking at a scene in the High Street from the 1920s is how little has changed over 70 years! Particularly striking are the roofs and windows, which remain almost identical. The White Hart Hotel has a new sign or two, and the greatest change seems to have been in the transport.
(Barbara Williams – Cricklade WI)

DILTON MARSH HIGH STREET

Dilton Marsh lies a few miles to the north-west of Warminster, and this view of the High Street at the beginning of the century shows a quiet village, dominated by the church on the right. The road was unmade and there were no pavements – but with so little traffic pedestrians were in very little danger.

(Maureen Flynn – Dilton Marsh WI)

Dilton Marsh High Street

Today the road seems to dominate the photograph, with its signs and clear markings. However, there have been remarkably few changes over the years in Dilton Marsh. It is still a village community with a heart that has evolved rather than been subjected to radical change, and the church still rises behind the houses just as it did a century and more ago.
(Maureen Flynn – Dilton Marsh WI)

The Cross, Downton

Downton's wide main street illustrates its importance as a market town in the past, and this sleepy scene from early in the century shows the old cross in the centre. There is an attractive row of thatched cottages on the left, with a little shop at the end of the row.

(Ruth Austen – Downton Afternoon WI)

The Cross, Downton

After the old cross disappeared, a new slightly smaller one was donated by the then owner of Fairfield House, Mrs Fisher. Today it stands at the centre of a car parking area. Some of the thatched cottages have gone, and in their place are modern houses and shops. The little shop at the end of the row is now a private house.
(Ruth Austen – Downton Afternoon WI)

East Knoyle

In the early years of the century Knoyle House stood on the approach to East Knoyle village, surrounded by parkland and rebuilt in 1881 by Alfred Seymour. The house was eventually demolished in 1955 after several unsuccessful attempts to sell it. Today (*inset*) gardens and a children's play area have taken its place. A bypass was opened in 1996 through the parkland to take heavy vehicles travelling to and from the Midlands, away from the village.
(Elizabeth Dobson – East Knoyle WI)

The Harp and Crown, Gastard

Gastard in 1904, when the old photograph was taken, had several shops including a post office and a bakery, now all gone. The village school closed in 1981. The Harp and Crown pub is still going strong though *(inset)*. The elm tree to the right has disappeared, but the tree on the left has only recently died and some of the same cottages are still standing. The farms employ few people nowadays and many villagers commute to local towns or London to work.

(Alan A'Court, Heather Williams – Gastard WI)

This photograph shows South Street, Great Wishford, and the church at the time of the First World War. The young baker's delivery boy was Leonard King, and he was sent out on his rounds with a two-wheeled covered cart and a large basket to take the bread to the back door. He would have been just one of the tradespeople who came regularly to the door and provided a personal service for the villagers.
(Christine Moulding – South Newton, Gt Wishford & Stapleford WI)

Today South Street looks very much the same, though telephone wires and television aerials are obvious additions to the scene. The houses are still mainly of flint and stone or brick with stone dressing, and have survived since the 17th or 18th centuries, as has the thatched cottage on the left. The old bakery, the last building on the left, is now the village store and post office.
(Christine Moulding – South Newton, Gt Wishford & Stapleford WI)

Idmiston

Idmiston village dates from Saxon times, and nestles in the Bourne valley in an area of outstanding natural beauty. These cottages in the village, seen here in the early 1900s, were built in 1879 on Earl Normanton's estate and were known as 58A and 58B High Street. Next to them stood a shoemaker's shop, the only one in the valley. The right-hand cottage was the home of the village blacksmith, whose forge was on the opposite side of the road.
(Dorothy Bailey – Idmiston & Porton WI)

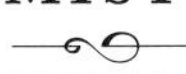

The little shoemaker's shop closed in 1910 and the building was demolished in 1972. The blacksmith too is long since gone, as is his forge. The cottage next to the shoemaker's was bought in 1929 by George White and became known as Vailley. Today it is modernised internally but externally remains very much as it was in 1879. The front gardens are very different, with room having to be made for cars!
(Dorothy Bailey – Idmiston & Porton WI)

West Street, Lacock

On the left, in this view of Lacock in 1910, is Mr Brinkworth's baker's shop, with his cart waiting outside. The large house facing down the street, one of the largest in Lacock, at this time was owned by a blacksmith, Mr Phelps but today is divided into two. Though tradesmen have changed (*inset*) much is outwardly the same, and the row of 18th century cottages has altered very little. The George inn has one of the longest continuously running licences in the country.
(Janet Burnett Brown – Lacock WI)

Laverstock

Laverstock lies on the outskirts of Salisbury and the population has increased dramatically over the century. The photographs show The Green, the focal point of the village, in the early 1920s and today (*inset*) though it has actually been moved a little to the right, to make way for the busy main road through the village. Despite the needs of modern parking, the charm of the scene still exists.
(Maureen Smith – Laverstock District Evening WI)

Crab Mill Cottage, Lea

Crab Mill Cottage, seen here in 1906, was originally one small cottage adjoining Crab Mill, which was a working mill from the 17th century until about 1938. It would have been the home of the miller. It was extended in 1832 and became two cottages. The cottages and mill spanned Woodbridge Brook and the area was known as Piggy Lea because of a large pig farm across the lane, which no longer exists!
(Pat. Mann – Lea WI)

Crab Mill Cottage, Lea

Today's owners have modernised the cottage, now one residence as is the Mill, but have not spoilt its historic appearance. The style of dress is very different – from the long skirts of yesterday to the casual clothes of today! Many villagers walk by the mill and on across the fields to Malmesbury, just as they have done since the 17th century.
(Pat Mann – Lea WI)

Limpley Stoke

Limpley Stoke is built on a hillside reaching down into the beautiful Avon valley. Middle Stoke, as its name implies, is halfway down. This photograph dates from 1920 and shows, on the left, the village school (1845) and opposite, the Baptist chapel (1888). Beyond is a row of 16th-century weavers' cottages and, in the distance, a cottage with smoke curling from the chimney. *(Ryliva Harrison – Limpley Stoke WI)*

Today's photograph shows the same buildings with the addition of the white telephone exchange, now unused, obscuring the distant cottages. The school with extensions is now the well-used village hall. The chapel is a private residence; the facade was kept but moved back several feet. The children and adults are all local residents, and their attire is so different to that of yesteryear. Less welcome changes are the overhead wires and parked cars!
(Ryliva Harrison – Limpley Stoke WI)

Park Farm, Lydiard Tregoze

In 1896, when this photograph was taken, the occupiers of Park Farm at Lydiard Tregoze were the Kinchin family. At the end of the house can be seen a small weeping ash tree, fashionable at that time. In the background is the thatched barn, and beside it the ricks, built on staddle-stones to keep the rats out. Perhaps the pony and trap was off to Swindon, three miles away.
(Sheila Rumming – Hook & District WI)

Park Farm, Lydiard Tregoze

The Rumming family became tenants of Park Farm in 1916, later buying it when the Bolingbroke Estate was sold in the 1940s, and they remain the owners today. The barn has been re-roofed in asbestos, which has saved the timber frame inside, and the redundant staddle-stones are roadside ornaments. Swindon is now only half a mile away and old timers would be astounded at the amount of traffic that speeds past on this once quiet country lane.
(Sheila Rumming – Hook & District WI)

The changing face of Odstock is apparent from this photograph taken c1917 of Homington Road. The house in the foreground was occupied by the two Compton brothers, and opposite lived their sister – out of a family of ten children! Today (*inset*) a modern house stands in its place. Glebe House at the end was built about 1625. Oliver Cromwell is thought to have been billeted here during the Civil War – and there is talk of his ghost appearing!
(Angela Moules – Odstock, Nunton & Bodenham WI)

Odstock

A water mill once stood on the River Ebble, and a spindle ran from the wheelhouse across the road, driving the water to the tithe barn opposite. This was later converted into a model dairy, said to have been one of the finest in the South of England. Sadly it burned down in the 1970s. The old wall links old and new, beside the modern house of today (*inset*).
(Angela Moules – Odstock, Nunton & Bodenham WI)

River Street, Pewsey

The Vale of Pewsey lies between Marlborough Downs and Salisbury Plain with Pewsey at its agricultural heart. In this photograph taken c1910 two little girls sharing secrets by the signpost in River Street are the only people in sight! Nearby on this neat and prosperous high street, an early garage offers cars for hire as well as oil and petrol. The thatched cottages called Phoenix Row were built in 1823.

(Pewsey Heritage Centre via Pewsey WI)

River Street, Pewsey

The monument of King Alfred was erected in 1913 to celebrate George V's coronation two years earlier, and in this photo it is decked with scaffolding in preparation for the carnival that has taken place every September in the town since 1898. Otherwise very little has changed along River Street – the garage is now a small housing development but the thatched cottages and the Phoenix Hotel beyond them are still going strong.
(Marie Neyroud – Pewsey WI)

STATION ROAD, PURTON

Station Road, Purton has not changed much since the 1900s – except for the traffic! Then, Purton was linked by a railway line, with a passenger and goods station. Now, sadly, the station has gone but trains still pass through beneath the bridge that forms part of Station Road. On the right lived the village blacksmith, but today *(inset)* it is a smart hairdresser's.
(Miriam Saunders – Purton Evening WI)

QUIDHAMPTON

At Quidhampton, in the Nadder valley, the 17th-century thatched house shown here, left, c1914 had in the century before been used as an overflow parish workhouse. In 1964 it was demolished and flats and bungalows built *(inset)*. Opposite lived the blacksmith, next door to his forge, but the forge and the creepers that clad his house have gone. Sadly, gone too are the oak, poplar and lime trees which lined the village street.
(Margaret King – Quidhampton WI)

Oxford Street, Ramsbury

This is a view that has remained charmingly unchanged since the beginning of the century, when Oxford Street, climbing gently out of the Kennet valley, once led to Ramsbury's village fields and pastures, now largely developed. Yet it must have been a bumpy ride for the child in that pram pushed by an older sister, over the cobbles and the unmade roadway. Another girl appears to be wearing a small top hat!
(Joyce Rosier – Ramsbury WI)

Oxford Street, Ramsbury

Today the curving downhill path still shows the thatched cottages to advantage. Although depleted in number, they have largely survived the several fires to which many on the other side of the street fell victim. In their place is a mixture of housing styles, blending with and complementing each other, down to The Square and High Street beyond. Walking down the street the eye is led to the view of the rolling green hills on the far side of the valley.
(Lois Smith – Ramsbury WI)

The Old Forge, Redlynch

On 27th January 1912 Mr Jabez Harrison received a Certificate of Registration from the Worshipful Company of Farriers, and this early photograph shows him standing in the doorway of his forge at Redlynch. The flat stone circle in front of the forge was where iron rims could be fitted to wooden wheels, and other tools of his trade, such as the grindstone, can be seen in the forge yard.
(Phyllis Brabrook – Redlynch WI)

The Old Forge, Redlynch

After Mr Harrison's retirement his son Horace, who was a master builder, used the forge in his work. However, in the 1980s the old forge was dismantled and rebuilt and an electrical shop was opened, still running today. Cars are now parked where the old cart once stood in the corner of the yard.
(Phyllis Brabrook – Redlynch WI)

This ordinary looking house in Rodbourne Cheney in 1900 was Elm Cottage, where the child murderer Mrs Dyer is reputed to have lived. Legend has it she would foster orphaned children from the village, but if they became too troublesome or expensive she would dispose of them in newly dug graves in the churchyard opposite. Mrs Dyer was hanged at Newgate in 1896 for child murders in the Reading area.
(Lesley Chambers – Greenmeadow & Haydon Wick WI)

Cheney Manor Road, Rodbourne Cheney

Elm Cottage was demolished in 1931 when the road was widened. A church hall was built on the site but was pulled down in 1995 and the development of houses shown in today's photograph was built. Rodbourne Cheney has changed a great deal since Mrs Dyer's day, and is now a part of Swindon.
(Lesley Chambers – Greenmeadow & Haydon Wick WI)

A Family Shop, Salisbury

The family-run corner shop has been one of the casualties of our change in shopping habits over the century. Mr Chapman came to Salisbury in 1900 and took over this shop on the corner of Nelson Road, until his death in 1927. The building had originally been designed as a hotel but ended up as a grocery business. During the war it withstood a bomb dropped just 50 yards away. It remained in the family until 1984, and the property was finally sold in 1997.
(Pat Chapman – Sarum WI)

Bishopdown Farm, Salisbury

In the early 1900s at Bishopdown Farm on London Road, the cows wait to be attended to in front of the barn, where the harvester, baler and other implements were kept during the winter. The farmhouse was to the left, out of view. Today the barn has been made into three houses, the farm was sold for building and up to this time nearly 500 houses have been built there. Thank goodness for memories!
(Sue Goodridge – Laverstock & Ford WI)

Salisbury Ring Road

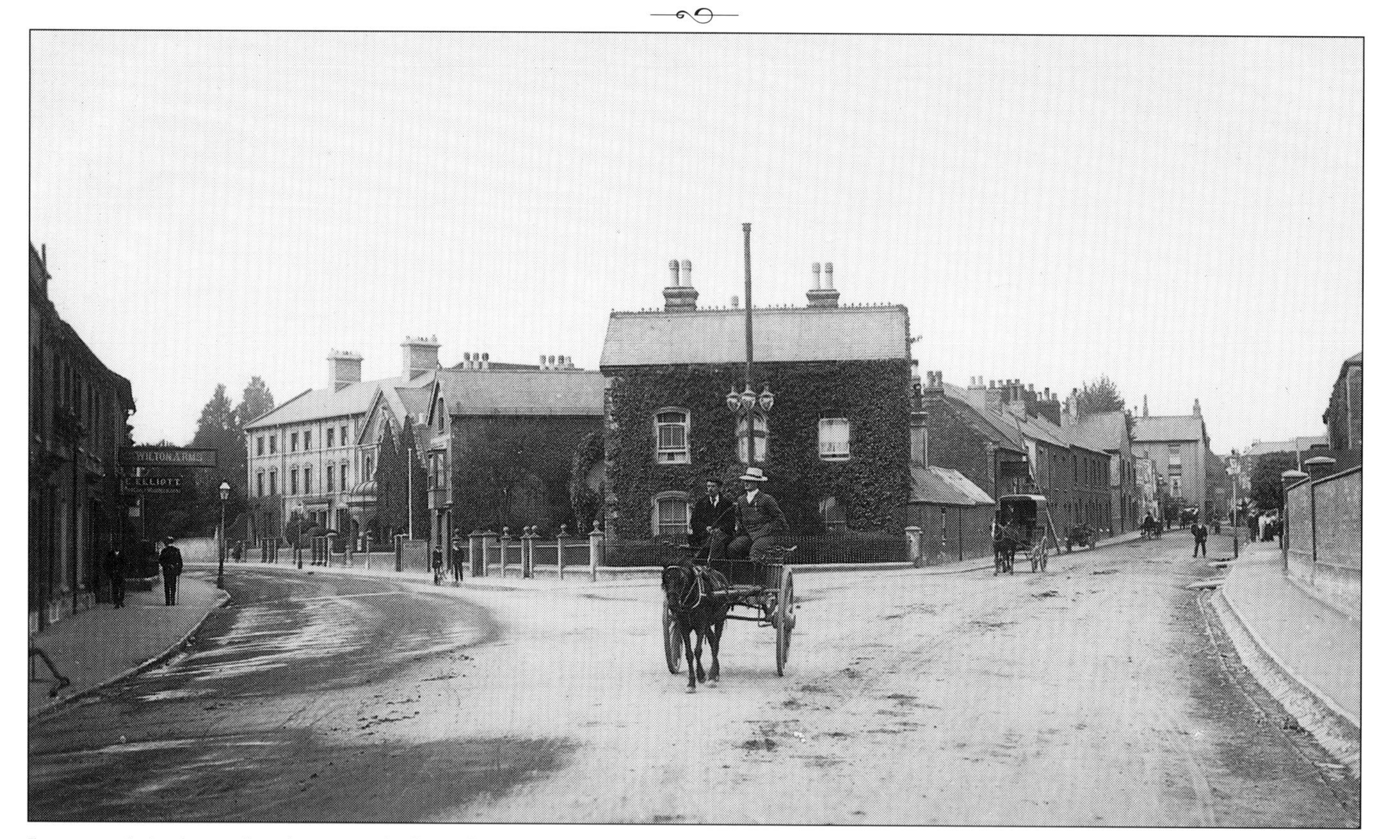

Laverstock is situated only one mile from Salisbury and local people are very familiar with the location of these two photographs. In 1916 it was time for a leisurely trip along the Wilton and Devizes roads – no haste, very little traffic to be seen and all of it horse-drawn!

(Maureen Smith – Laverstock District Evening WI)

Today it is all hustle and speed by this very busy roundabout on the main Salisbury ring road, and the motor car reigns supreme. The ivy clad building in the centre of the old photograph was demolished to make way for a necessary petrol service station, but the three-storey buildings and chapel to the rear still remain in their original form.
(Maureen Smith – Laverstock District Evening WI)

The Old Ironworks, Seend

This photograph of the Seend Ironworks was taken over a century ago from the Barge Bridge in the Cleeve, Seend. Iron from the nearby quarries was first smelted there in January 1860, until the ironworks were demolished in 1889. Mr Oliver Kimber, in the top hat, was the Clerk in charge of the ironworks and he subsequently purchased the site.
(Betty Smith – Seend WI)

The Old Ironworks, Seend

Today there is nothing of the past to be seen from the parapet of the Barge Bridge! Iron ore continued to be quarried from the site until 1946 but today Nature has covered the scars of industry and it is hard to believe that such an industrious scene ever took place here. In very wet weather the site becomes flooded and is home to a family of ducks.
(Betty Smith – Seend WI)

Semley Village Street

Perhaps the most noticeable changes in Semley over the century have been around the church of St Leonard. This photograph taken in 1904 shows a horse and cart belonging to Mr Chubb, the butcher. Today *(inset)* both it and the thatched cottages are gone. Grazing was allowed on the common then, but no longer. The cottages became buildings that served as a post office and cobbler's shop, but are now one private house.
(Margaret O'Donovan – Semley WI)

The Bennet Arms, Semley

The Bennet Arms was built in 1596 and has served as an inn ever since. At the turn of the century there was a small shop alongside. Now that extension has been absorbed into the main building, and the white walls offer a more cheerful welcome than the creeper-covered stone of 1900. The car and the fashions have changed somewhat over the years too!
(Phyllis. Jelbart – Semley WI)

Sherston High Street

This photograph of Sherston High Street was taken c1905, just after the water tap was erected in the road for the use of villagers. The building on the left, with the little oval window, is one of the oldest in the village and the balcony over the porch was used by the auctioneer on market day. There was also a market office in the Tolsey, on the right, and a blacksmith's shop. There were four inns in the High Street, with three others elsewhere in the village!
(Jean Poole – Sherston WI)

Sherston High Street

There has been little change in the centre of the village, though larger estates have been built on the outskirts, and the population is still about the same at 1,500. The Tolsey was completely altered in the 1920s and in its long life has been a youth hostel, a prisoner of war hospital, and a doctors' surgery! The inns have all found other uses, from a butcher's shop to a computer software manufacturer's. The village school, over 150 years old, is still in use.
(Jean Poole – Sherston WI)

Southwick Old Forge

The building that housed the old forge at Southwick was originally a Wesleyan chapel, in Wesley Lane. In the 1800s it became the blacksmith's house and forge. In the photograph are Mr Holland, the blacksmith, and Mr Amer, his assistant.
(Olive Blissett – Southwick WI)

Southwick Old Forge

Today the Old Forge is a private house and shows little to indicate its busy past life. Blacksmiths found that the advent of the motor car gradually robbed them of their place at the heart of a rural community. Though some still thrive today where there is a strong riding tradition or where wrought iron work has brought them new customers, many an old forge, like the one at Southwick, has long since disappeared.
(Olive Blissett – Southwick WI)

Stapleford Village Street

In 1905 a photograph of Fete Day at Stapleford captured a glimpse of a self-sufficient village. There was a butcher who delivered around the area, a baker, a cobbler, a blacksmith, a coalman, a builder and a thatcher. The village also had a school, a post office, a general store and a public house, the whole watched over by two policemen.
(Lorna Scott – South Newton, Gt Wishford & Stapleford WI)

Stapleford Village Street

Today Stapleford still has its pretty thatched cottages, and the pub and post office, plus a garage with a small shop and an occasional passing police car! Stapleford lies eight miles north-west of Salisbury, and while there are some newer houses, there are still many fine old houses and cottages here. The spirit of the community survives, even though the Fete Day did not.
(Lorna Scott – South Newton, Gt Wishford & Stapleford WI)

Steeple Ashton's Old Village Pond

Steeple Ashton is an ancient village a few miles east of Trowbridge. In the early years of the century there was a village pond situated beside the High Street, and the photograph shows Church Farm and Tylers Farm beyond, with a thatched house opposite. The pond was used amongst other things for watering stock, and during hot dry weather many a cart would stop a while to soak its wheels to stop the wood shrinking.
(Ann Ferry – Steeple Ashton WI)

Steeple Ashton's Old Village Pond

Steeple Ashton's village pond was filled in during 1922, following the death from diphtheria of a young girl who lived opposite. Today the scene is quite different. The house on the right of the road now has a tiled roof and there are a number of telegraph poles and some street lighting to be seen. Trees have been planted which obscure the view of the two farmhouses, and a brick wall and grass verge have replaced the pond.
(Ann Ferry – Steeple Ashton WI)

Sutton Benger High Street

In 1918, when this photograph was taken, most of the properties in Sutton Benger were still owned by the Draycot Estate. Clearly visible on the left along the High Street is the butcher's shop, which unfortunately was demolished in the late 1970s and an ornamental garden wall erected.

(Kay Taylor – Sutton Benger WI)

Changes to the street scene today in Sutton Benger include the provision of lighting, telegraph poles and road signs, and the addition of a proper pedestrian footpath. The High Street was once part of the busy A420 but the M4 motorway in the 1970s provided welcome relief from some of the heavy traffic, and in the late 1980s the road was downgraded to a B-road.
(Kay Taylor – Sutton Benger WI)

HIGH STREET, UPAVON

Upavon nestles in the Pewsey Vale, on the edge of Salisbury Plain. In these photographs of the High Street, the difference in the road surface is obvious but otherwise much remains the same as at the turn of the century. The little cycle shop is gone, replaced by a new house, but next door the large timbered house, one of the oldest in Upavon, has been restored.
(Mary Parsons-Hann – Upavon WI)

Jarvis Street, Upavon

The road surface of Jarvis Street at Upavon, made up of cracked stone in 1910, is also an apparent change over the century, and the provision of a clearly defined pavement for pedestrians, so necessary with today's traffic. Here though, as in the High Street, the old cottages are still standing.
(Mary Parsons-Hann – Upavon WI)

Loves Lane, Wingfield

Loves Lane is situated in the delightful little village of Wingfield. It was so called after a family called Love who lived there for many generations. The old pump at the top of the lane was used by all the householders before water was laid on – and electricity did not come until the late 1940s. There were no back entrances to the cottages, so all deliveries were through the front door, even coal, which was kept in a cupboard under the stairs.
(Betty Webb – Wingfield WI)

Loves Lane, Wingfield

The last of the Love family died in 1970 and the cottages were then bought by a local vet who modernised them and let them out as rented homes. The lane has changed, but not much in appearance. The allotments opposite have been fenced off and there is a modern chalet bungalow there now, while the old coach house has been converted into a delightful new house. The old pump has been removed.
(Betty Webb – Wingfield WI)

WINTERBOURNE DAUNTSEY GARAGE

By the time this photograph of Winterbourne Dauntsey was taken in the 1940s the motor car had made its mark on village life. The village lies on the A338 into Salisbury and many a car would have pulled in here for service by the family who ran the business from the beginning of the century. The petrol pumps look very old-fashioned to modern eyes, and the old red telephone box was in use – with the pushchair left happily outside in those quiet times.
(Muriel Godbold – Bourne Valley WI)

Winterbourne Dauntsey Garage

The family ceased to run the petrol pumps in the late 1960s, but they still own the property in Winterbourne Dauntsey. The pumps have gone, and so has the red telephone box, and the garage now concentrates on car sales and repairs.
(Muriel Godbold – Bourne Valley WI)

Wootton Bassett High Street

This view of Wootton Bassett's High Street and Town Hall was taken in about 1910. Then, part of the large building on the left was the Royal Oak and Watts' shop, shared with Bevirs' offices on the corner. Soon after this photograph was taken it ceased to be an inn and during the First World War housed prisoners of war, before becoming so delapidated that it had to be pulled down.
(Beryl Prentice – Wootton Bassett Afternoon WI)

The High Street today is modernised, with wider pavements and seats. The old town hall has been restored to its original (1690) design, unfortunately not with everyone's approval. The Royal Oak, of course, is long gone and part of the grounds are now a supermarket. Watts' shop became the Midland Bank branch in 1924. Bevirs' offices have stayed the same and help to bridge the gap over the century.
(Beryl Prentice – Wootton Bassett Afternoon WI)

Acknowledgements

Contributions for this collection were received from the following Institutes, and although for reasons of space not every photograph could be included, without them all this book could not have been produced:

All Cannings • Etchilhampton & Allington
Ashton Keynes • Avebury & District • Baydon
Biddlestone & Hartham • Bishopstone with
Hinton Parva • Bourne Valley • Bowerchalke
Box • Boxlea • Bremhill & District • Brinkworth
Bromham • Burbage • Chapmanslade • Christian
Malford & Foxham • Codford • Collingbourne
Kingston • Corsley • Cortington • Cricklade
Dilton Marsh • Downton Afternoon • East
Knoyle • Gastard • Greenmeadow & Haydon
Wick • Hardenhuish • Harnham • Hook &
District • Idmiston & Porton • Lacock
Laverstock & Ford • Laverstock Evening • Lea
Limpley Stoke • Odstock, Nunton & Bodenham
Pewsey • Potterne • Purton Evening
Quidhampton • Ramsbury • Redlynch • Sarum
Seend • Semley • Sherston • South Newton,
Great Wishford & Stapletord • Southwick
Steeple Ashton • Sutton Benger • Upavon
Wingfield • Wootton Bassett Afternoon.

Cover Photos: Chapmanslade is a linear village close to Salisbury Plain. With the exception of the electricity and telephone-carrying telegraph pole, and the appearance of the road (then cared for by the local stone-cracker) there seems little difference in the photos taken nearly a century apart. Then, the village was self-sufficient in trades and services, but today it has just one of three churches, one of four pubs and no shop or post office – fortunately the village school, over 100 years old, continues to thrive. *(Susan Waterman – Chapmanslade WI)*